Looking at . . . Psittacosaurus
A Dinosaur from the CRETACEOUS Period

THE NEW DINOSAUR COLLECTION

For a free color catalog describing Gareth Stevens' list of high-quality books, call 1-800-542-2595 (USA) or 1-800-461-9120 (Canada). Gareth Stevens' Fax: (414) 225-0377.

Library of Congress Cataloging-in-Publication Data available upon request from publisher. Fax: (414) 225-0377 for the attention of the Publishing Records Department.

ISBN 0-8368-1348-0

This North American edition first published in 1995 by
Gareth Stevens Publishing
1555 North RiverCenter Drive, Suite 201
Milwaukee, Wisconsin 53212 USA

This U.S. edition © 1995 by Gareth Stevens, Inc. Created with original © 1995 by Quartz Editorial Services, Premier House, 112 Station Road, Edgware HA8 7AQ U.K.

Consultant: Dr. David Norman, Director of the Sedgwick Museum of Geology, University of Cambridge, England.

Additional artwork by Clare Herronneau.

Printed in the United States of America

1 2 3 4 5 6 7 8 9 99 98 97 96 95

Looking at . . . Psittacosaurus
A Dinosaur from the CRETACEOUS Period

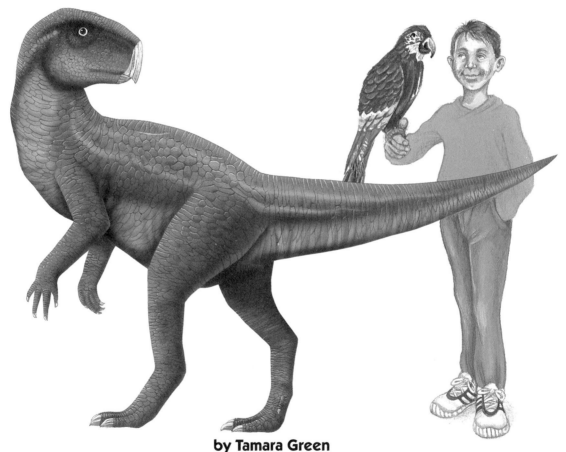

by Tamara Green

Illustrated by Tony Gibbons

THE NEW
DINOSAUR
COLLECTION

Gareth Stevens Publishing
MILWAUKEE

Contents

5 Introducing **Psittacosaurus**

6 Beaked herbivore

8 Small, slim skeleton

10 Wonderful find!

12 Dinosaurs from China

14 Eating habits

16 Uncertain fate

18 Cretaceous survivors

20 **Psittacosaurus** data

22 Other beaked dinosaurs

24 Glossary and Index

Introducing
Psittacosaurus

When did **Psittacosaurus** live? Where have its remains been found? Who were its enemies? And what did it eat?

You'll find the answers to these and many other questions as you read all about this curious creature.

From its head alone, **Psittacosaurus** (<u>SIT</u>-AK-OH-<u>SAW</u>-RUS) looked as if it might have belonged to the parrot family. But, as you are about to discover, it had no feathers or wings; stood about your height; and was, of course, a dinosaur!

You'll also discover some creatures alive today whose ancestors roamed planet Earth way back in **Psittacosaurus**'s Cretaceous time.

5

Beaked herbivore

The strangest thing about **Psittacosaurus** was its horny, toothless beak. It looked like a parrot's beak and was used for chopping plants and tough leaves.

So it should not come as any surprise to learn that its name actually means "parrot reptile."

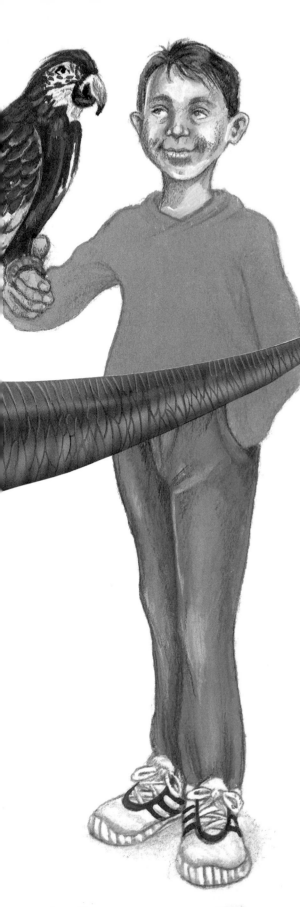

If you could have looked inside its mouth, you would have seen that **Psittacosaurus** had teeth only at the sides of its beak. It needed these for chewing its food.

It was only about 5 feet (1.5 meters) long and quite small for a dinosaur. It weighed just 50 pounds (22 kilograms). So it may not have seemed as fierce or frightening as some other dinosaurs.

Look how short its arms were in comparison to its legs! On each hand, **Psittacosaurus** had four fingers. These were suited for grabbing twigs and other vegetation.

There were three main toes on each foot, with one extra, smaller toe. Notice how the tail was fairly thick and tapered toward the tip. **Psittacosaurus** probably held this up level with its body when running.

Did you know that many scientists now believe that birds evolved from dinosaurs? Only a few prehistoric creatures looked like birds — but, with its prominent beak, **Psittacosaurus**'s head certainly had a similarity!

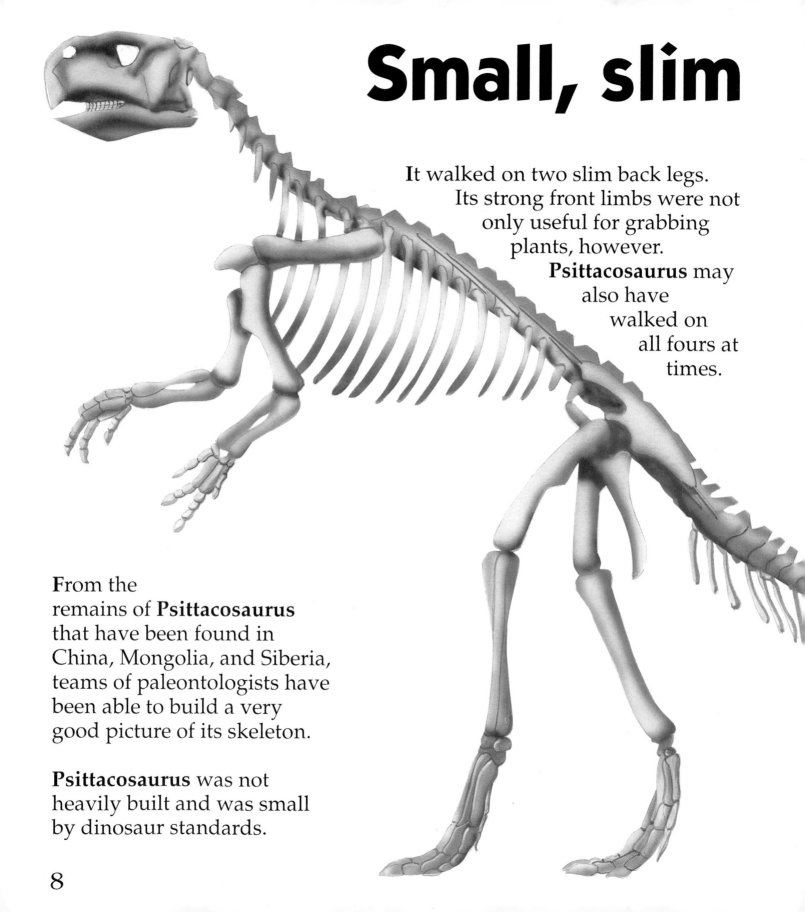

Small, slim

It walked on two slim back legs. Its strong front limbs were not only useful for grabbing plants, however. **Psittacosaurus** may also have walked on all fours at times.

From the remains of **Psittacosaurus** that have been found in China, Mongolia, and Siberia, teams of paleontologists have been able to build a very good picture of its skeleton.

Psittacosaurus was not heavily built and was small by dinosaur standards.

8

skeleton

There were four clawed fingers on its forelimbs and four toes on each foot.

Those slim back legs may have helped **Psittacosaurus** move if chased by a predator that was out for the kill.

Now take a look at **Psittacosaurus**'s head. Its skull was chunky, with a large, sharp, parrotlike beak that had a curved lower part to it. Its eyes and nostrils were high on its head.

There was also a ridge at the back of the head.

This ridge gave support to the jaw muscles. Although hardly noticeable, it was a miniature version of the frill that dinosaurs such as **Triceratops** (TRY-SER-A-TOPS) had.

Psittacosaurus could move its neck quite easily, which must have been useful for reaching the foliage it ate. A flexible neck also meant it could turn its head to watch for enemies if it caught the scent or sound of one.

A few years ago, a leading paleontologist noticed some very small skulls among **Psittacosaurus** bones discovered in the 1920s. These probably belonged to **Psittacosaurus** babies, about the length of your arm from fingertip to elbow. There were worn teeth, however. This showed these tiny babies were probably already feeding themselves rather than still being fed by a parent.

In the early 1920s, the American paleontologist Henry F. Osborn suggested an expedition to Mongolia. His aim was to find out how humankind had first developed. At the time, many scientists thought the human race had first evolved in that part of Asia.

Alas, they did not succeed. In fact, they found no interesting human remains at all. But the expedition had not been a waste of time or money. What Osborn and his team did discover accidentally were the remains of several new dinosaurs, and among them was **Psittacosaurus**! It must have lived in a landscape very much like the one shown here.

Soon scientists were digging up what seemed a huge and very rich Cretaceous dinosaur "graveyard." There were lots of bones and skulls, as well as fossilized eggs and nests. Many of Osborn's finds are now in the American Museum of Natural History in New York City, which has the world's largest dinosaur collection.

11

Dinosaurs from China

1

Gasosaurus lived before
Psittacosaurus in Jurassic times.
It was about 13 feet (4 m) long
and 8 feet (2.5 m) high —
taller than a
fully grown
human being —
and had nasty
fangs for stabbing
and cutting
at flesh.

The Beijing Natural History
Museum houses reconstructions of
several important finds that have
been made in China. Among them
is **Psittacosaurus** (**1**), and it is in
good company.

Gasosaurus (GAS-OH-SAW-RUS) (**2**)
has a name that means
"gas lizard" because
of the help
given by the
petroleum industry
when **Gasosaurus** was
discovered a few years ago.

2

Mamenchisaurus
(MA-MENCH-IH-SAW-RUS) (**3**)
was also from Jurassic
times, but was a
herbivore like
Psittacosaurus. Scientists think it
may have had one of the longest
necks of all the dinosaurs —
perhaps 50 feet (15 m) of neck
alone, taking up almost half of its
89-foot (27-m)-long body.

Just imagine what
you would look like if
your neck were half the
length of your body!

Shantungosaurus
(SHAN-TOONG-OH-SAW-
RUS) (**4**) was another plant-eater,
but from Cretaceous times. Its
body was about as long as
Mamenchisaurus's neck alone.
It had a flat head and toothless
beak; hooflike nails on its toes;
and a thick, tapering tail.

Experts think **Tsintaosaurus**
(SIN-TAO-SAW-RUS) (**5**), another
plant-eater from the Cretaceous
age, was about 33 feet (10 m)
long – that's about
six times your
body length.
It had a tall
spike rising from
its duck-billed
head.

As you can
see, there
is plenty of variety
in the many
types
of dinosaurs
that have been
discovered in
China so far!

13

Eating habits

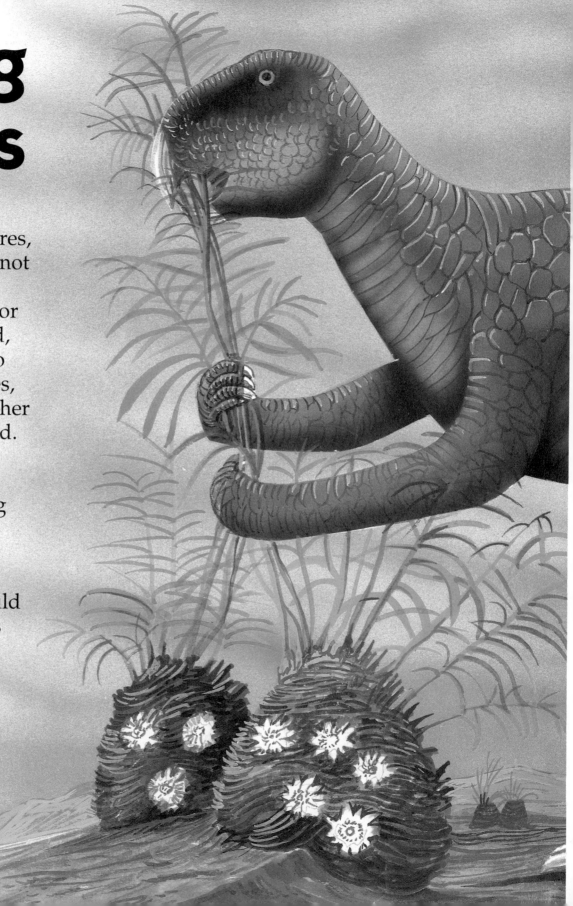

Like all the herbivores, **Psittacosaurus** did not touch meat and so was not a predator or a scavenger. Instead, it looked forward to meals of crisp leaves, fresh shoots, and other nutritious plant food. Its beak was very useful; it was ideal for cutting or slicing through all sorts of tough vegetation.

Psittacosaurus would snip off large pieces and then use the teeth at the sides of its mouth to chomp them up for swallowing.

It would have used the muscles in its cheeks, as well as its tongue, to help with this.

Some scientists think there may have been a gizzard to help with processing these lumps of food so they could be easily digested. A gizzard is a special part of the stomach, now found in birds, where hard food is broken up.

Over one hundred stones, known as *gastroliths*, have been found in the skeleton of a **Psittacosaurus**. These would have been swallowed to help with the grinding of food in the dinosaur's stomach so it could thoroughly digest its meals of tough plants.

Uncertain fate

It was a stormy day in Early Cretaceous times. Groups of **Psittacosaurus** had taken shelter from the heavy rain under huge trees. Now that the rain had almost stopped, however, they ventured

These grunting noises came from the **Psittacosaurus** as they stopped to digest their meal. From time to time, too, the flapping and screeching of pterosaurs could be heard overhead.

out to feed on low-lying plants and shrubs.

The thunder had died down and all was calm again. The only sounds were occasional background snorts.

It was just as well that the **Psittacosaurus** were small. This meant they did not have to compete with the **Wuerhosaurus** (WER-HO-SAW-RUS) that were busy browsing in the same area. The **Wuerhosaurus** could reach up to higher branches for leaves.

The **Wuerhosaurus** — 20-foot (6-m)-long, four-legged plant-eaters — had smaller heads than **Psittacosaurus** and two rows of plates along their backs. They had nasty tail spikes, too — useful whenever they needed to fight in self-defense against marauding predators.

Quick as a flash, they began to scamper away, just as a dreadful roar and thudding footsteps started to resound through the valley.

Would these herbivores escape to survive another Cretaceous day? Or would one, or more, fall

But most of the time they were busy feeding on plants.

Suddenly, all the herbivores stopped what they were doing and sniffed the air. They could sense the approach of a meat-eater. Instinctively, they knew there was no time to lose.

victim to a giant carnivore's terrible teeth and savage bite?

Life for plant-eaters 140 million years ago was generally peaceful. But they were always at risk from fierce and hungry carnivores that relished fresh dinosaur flesh and that killed daily for meals.

Cretaceous survivors

Dinosaurs died out 65 million years ago, at the end of Cretaceous times. There are, however, some creatures in the world today whose ancestors also roamed Earth at the same time as some of the dinosaurs. One of these is the crocodile, which probably looked then very much like it does now. But, unlike today's crocodiles — most of which live in rivers — it lived in the warm seas, alongside huge, prehistoric, long-necked sea reptiles.

Cretaceous waters were rich with life. There is fossil evidence of aquatic reptiles such as turtles, for instance, and also amphibians (creatures living on land but breeding in water) such as frogs and salamanders.

On land, meanwhile, there were small mammals that looked like the voles we know today, as well as various types of snakes and lizards.

There were creatures that resembled hedgehogs and shrews, too. And now that there were flowering plants — such as magnolias, holly, and climbing roses — bees and other insects of the Cretaceous world would have helped pollinate them.

By Late Cretaceous times, there were also a few birds, some of which looked like the herons and terns that are familiar to us now.

But the many kinds of birds we have today started to evolve only after dinosaurs became extinct.

Psittacosaurus data

Psittacosaurus was smaller than an average, fully grown adult. So do you think it would have made a good household pet if humans had existed all those millions of years ago? Take a look at its principal features, and then decide.

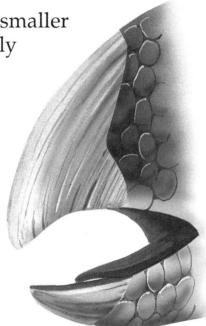

Lower beak bone

Experts are now convinced that even though it did not have a frill or horns, **Psittacosaurus** must have been an early type of **Ceratopsid**. A special type of bone has been found in its beak. This is known as the rostral bone, and so far only **Ceratopsids** have it.

Parrotlike beak

Made of bone with a horny covering, **Psittacosaurus**'s beak grew continually. This meant that it did not get worn down as a result of repeated cutting at plants. If annoyed by a predator, it might have given quite a nip with its beak, too.

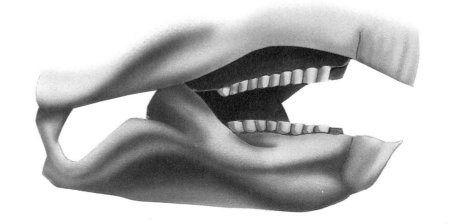

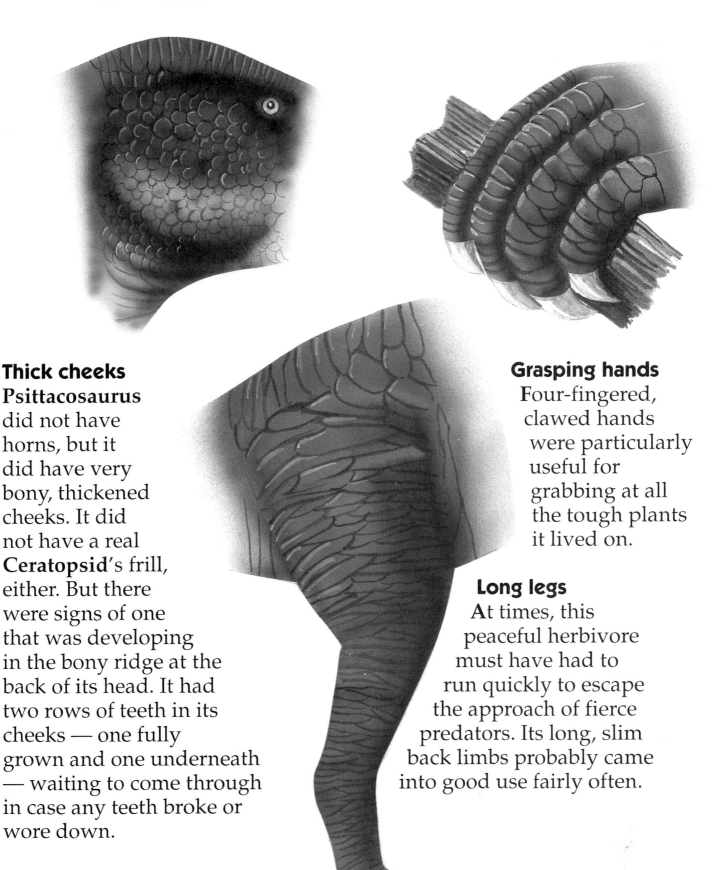

Thick cheeks
Psittacosaurus did not have horns, but it did have very bony, thickened cheeks. It did not have a real **Ceratopsid**'s frill, either. But there were signs of one that was developing in the bony ridge at the back of its head. It had two rows of teeth in its cheeks — one fully grown and one underneath — waiting to come through in case any teeth broke or wore down.

Grasping hands
Four-fingered, clawed hands were particularly useful for grabbing at all the tough plants it lived on.

Long legs
At times, this peaceful herbivore must have had to run quickly to escape the approach of fierce predators. Its long, slim back limbs probably came into good use fairly often.

21

Other beaked dinosaurs

Scientists believe
Psittacosaurus (**1**), from
Early Cretaceous times,
was an early relative of
the **Ceratopsids** – dinosaurs
with horns, beaks,
and frills.

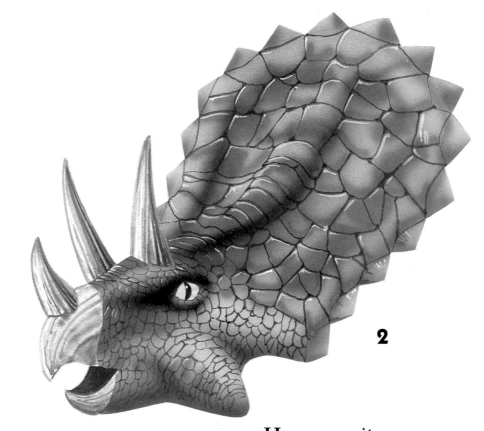

1

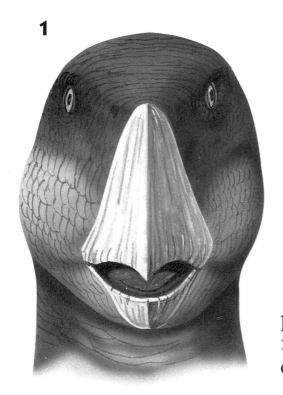

2

However, it
was much more lightly built. And,
although it had a beak, it had no real
neck frill or large horns like Late
Cretaceous **Triceratops** (**2**), which was
a true **Ceratopsid**. So **Psittacosaurus**
probably appeared on Earth at a stage
in evolution from one group of
dinosaurs to another.

But quite a few other dinosaurs — all of them herbivores — that were not **Ceratopsids** also had beaks. Among them was **Ornithomimus** (OR-<u>NITH</u>-OH-<u>MIME</u>-US) **(3)**, whose name means "bird mimic."

A speedy runner, **Ornithomimus** looked like one of today's flightless birds, the ostrich, but had a long tail and no feathers, and, of course, could not fly. About 11 feet (3.5 m) long with a small head at the end of a long, *S*-shaped neck, it roamed what is now North America, and also Tibet, in Late Cretaceous times.

3

Dinosaurs such as Late Cretaceous **Edmontosaurus** (ED-<u>MONT</u>-OH-<u>SAW</u>-RUS) **(4)**, below, called by this name because its remains were found in Edmonton, Canada, also had a beak, but it was more like a duck's bill.

Unlike a duck, however, **Edmontosaurus** had hundreds of teeth that were farther back in its mouth. These were used for grinding vegetation.

4

With all the slicing and cutting work they had to do, you might think dinosaur beaks would have worn down. Not so! Amazingly, they continued to grow and were always in good shape for use.

GLOSSARY

carnivores — meat-eating animals.

evolve — to change shape or develop gradually over a long period of time.

extinction — the dying out of all members of a plant or animal species.

fangs — long, sharp teeth.

fossils — traces or remains of plants and animals found in rock.

herbivores — plant-eating animals.

paleontologists — scientists who study the remains of plants and animals that lived millions of years ago.

petroleum — oil found in the upper layers of Earth.

predators — animals that kill other animals for food.

remains — a skeleton, bones, or dead body.

scavengers — animals that eat the leftovers or carcasses of other animals.

INDEX

Ceratopsids 20, 21, 22, 23
Cretaceous Period 11, 16, 17, 18-19, 22, 23

dinosaur graveyards 11

Edmontosaurus 23
evolution 7, 11, 19, 22
extinction 19

foliage 9
fossils 18

Gasosaurus 12
gastroliths 15

herbivores 13, 14, 17, 21, 23

Jurassic Period 12, 13

Mamenchisaurus 13

Ornithomimus 23
Osborn, Henry F. 11

paleontologists 8, 9, 11
petroleum 12
predators 9, 14, 17, 20, 21
Psittacosaurus: back legs of 8, 21; and digestion 15; eating habits of 7, 14-15; forelimbs of 7, 8, 9, 21; head of 5, 9, 21; height of 5; as herbivore 6-7, 14, 21; length of 7; parrotlike beak of 6, 9, 14, 20; remains of 5, 8, 20; rostral bone of 20; skeleton of 8-9; tail of 7; teeth of 21; toes of 7, 9; weight of 7
pterosaurs 16

scavengers 14
scientists 7, 11, 15, 22
sea reptiles 18
Shantungosaurus 13

Triceratops 22
Tsintaosaurus 13

Wuerhosaurus 16, 17

24